Cryptocurrency

The Complete Insider Guide of Cryptocurrency and Lucrative Secret to Become Millionaire with this Money of the Future

In this book, you will learn about the ever-changing world of cryptocurrency. Digital currency is rather new, and has only been around for ten years, but is gaining traction and value every single day. We will simplify the complicated nature of this new financial market that is hitting every market on a global scale. Cryptocurrency is proving to be more and more noteworthy, because there is no limitation upon using this currency, well as long as it is accepted. Think of it as a global currency. You may have heard Bitcoin take off in the news, here in the year 2017, if you missed the Bitcoin train, it is not too late to start investing in cryptocurrency, you must begin to look at altcoins, and there you shall find a valuable alternative.

In this book, we will cover ways you can increase your investments and profits, by investing early on. Think about it this way, there are billions upon billions of people in the world; being that these digital coins can be used around the globe, this increases their valuable nature. The more billions of people who decide to adopt cryptocurrency, the more monetary profit an investor will create. There are plenty of ways to produce an income of course, but in this book, we will walk you through a path to make millions, but you have to be willing to invest research, time, effort, and money. The saying always stands true; you have to spend money to make money. But who said you have to spend a ton of money to be a millionaire? This is not always the case, and this is where new money millionaires come into the picture.

Do you think that working a normal nine to five job will create monetary wealth that you've always dreamed of? Sure, you need income to start with, but keeping this mindset will not help anyone grow into the next financial bracket. In fact, if you don't take it to your own account to intelligently invest, your life may be at a standstill. Keep in mind, stagnancy never helped anyone. Sure, go ahead and keep your nine to five job, but you might want to ask your boss for a raise if you want to 'slightly' get ahead. If you want to get ahead of the financial game, then you must take a risk, not just any risk, but a cryptocurrency risk. Years down the road, you and your family will be sitting on a golden nest egg of wealth that you created from believing in the digital currency era that is entering households, not just in the U.S. but in countries that have markets that are filled with billions of people.

Gain more net worth, and learn the truth about the digital market. Inside *Cryptocurrency*, you will find lucrative secrets that will set you up to be a millionaire. Since the cryptocurrency market is new, now is the time to learn about this rewarding investment before it is too late. Do yourself a favor today, and realize that the stock market is a bit stagnant these days, and begin to come to a realization that people are looking for faster growth and newer investments; digital currency is the new answer in the year 2018.

There has been speculation that Bitcoin will one day reach $100K USD or possibly even a million dollars! If this is the case, then we need to start researching new alternative coins, which are similar to Bitcoin, as similar currencies are being overlooked and are completely undervalued. Why not serve yourself a piece of the pie and start appreciating your finances now; today.

Inside we will teach you about how to buy cryptocurrencies, along with strategies to buy low, sell high, hold, and or make the best decisions before you buy into your new cryptocurrency portfolio. The tools are inside, all you have to do is patiently learn, read, and take heed of the advice that is given to help you advance into a world of new wealth.

Knowledge is always power in the financial arena and every aspect of life. Learn to be a millionaire in a matter of weeks and soon your investment accounts will rise. This book, also mentions information about individuals who have succeeded and those that have created their own demise, by not following proper legal rules that are set forth.

In this book, we will teach you that it is important to analyze pricing, this way when the price does happen to be right, you invest enough, and not too little. Investing too little is better than nothing, but if you want to be a millionaire, listen up, because investing in one or two coins is fine, but to reach the million dollar mark, you definitely want to buy more than that.

Innovation will continue to rule the world, it is about time that you stop being fearful of the future financial world that includes cryptocurrency. Take a big as a risk, as much as you are willing to lose. If you feel comfortable losing it all, then you have invested properly in cryptocurrency. Buying in early will ensure that you lock down discounted prices; the prices that the general population constantly yearns for. Make sure to have a tight watch on the daily coins and their profit/losses, by the day, the hour, and the month. Keep in mind, that just because Bitcoin is not price friendly at the moment, it could fall at any moment; so keep your ears and eyes open to all possibilities. As with cryptocurrencies the possibilities really are endless.

Remember not be complicit in your lifestyle, because you really can have it all, once you reach your investment goals. Securing your financial future starts with the decisions that you make today. Cryptocurrency has been able to turn millionaires into billionaires, put that idea into perspective.

People need to start realizing if they haven't already that blockchain technology is taking the complicated nature out of purchasing monetary value online. A worldwide currency will only change the world, second by second.

On one last note, before we get into the nuts and bolts of cryptocurrency, it is December 2017, and gold prices have gone down, while Bitcoin prices have surged, several analysts have made a correlation to the two. This fact proves that digital currency is becoming the new hot commodity, the same way our computers are essential to our major global corporations. If it wasn't for technology, our jobs would suffer, hence creating a large unemployment gap around the globe. The same way we need oil to run our cars, cryptocurrency is just as important to computers, trading, and finance.

Now strap on to your seats, because the cryptocurrency market has been known to take off faster than any stock, option, or bond around. Grab a comfortable location, and learn all you can about the new digital market that will soon give you the freedom that you've always dreamed of. Stop working for money, and start by putting your money to work for you. We all work hard for our money, it is about time we stop working so hard and start working smart. With the tools inside of *Cryptocurrency,* you will soon be grateful you decided to give this book a read.

Remember to read as much information as you possibly can, otherwise, you will be left in the cold and your crypto coins will be oversold—if you wait too long. There's no better time than today, to invest in a new and improved market. Going green a.k.a electronic never seemed so smart than in the year 2017. Blockchain technology is taking off and there is no stopping it now that the beginning has come to fruition. Expand your income by learning everything there is to know about *Cryptocurrency, the* money of the future.

The secrets inside of this book will ensure that you can become a millionaire if you implement the strategies that we have provided for you. Next, it is up to you to decide if the pros outweighs the risks. There has never been a better time to take a new opportunity with future assets that will not only benefit you, but will prove to be beneficial for your family, and generations into the future—all because you decided to make a smart investing decision. Just think about it, there are billions of people out there and billions of devices that people use, second by second, you owe it to yourself to not only believe in technology, but to believe in digital currency. Stay safe, invest well, and know that if you are going to put your information out there, you must protect it with layers and layers of security.

Becoming a millionaire starts with a mindset and ends with an action at the right time. Don't think of cryptocurrency and correlate this type of digital currency to the stock exchange, sure there are some similarities, but digital finance is just the beginning; a completely different ball game. Protection of assets could not be stressed enough. Once you start realizing that you are actually investing in the technology itself, then you will be sure to feel much more secure about your financially sound decision, though the market is completely radical 24/7, you now have an opportunity the make unlimited amounts of money. We wish you a future full of monetary abundance. Enjoy.

TABLE OF CONTENTS:

What Is Cryptocurrency and How Does It Work? 16

Coin Lovers 25

The Blockchain Bubble 29

Population Equals Billions! 35

Top Cryptocurrency To Buy In 2017 38

Professional Platforms To Exchange Cryptocurrency and How They Work 42

When To Buy and When To Sell Cryptocurrency? 45

What Kinds of Currencies Are Counting As Cryptocurrency, Which One Have Biggest Impact Such As Bitcoin, etc.? 51

How To Minimize Risks With Trading and Investing Cryptocurrency 55

Mistakes To Avoid When Trading and Investing Cryptocurrency For Beginners And Advanced ..58

15 Effective Strategies or Effective Ways To Make Money With Cryptocurrency and Become A Millionaire 60

The Terminologies Related To Cryptocurrency 68

How Government and Financial Services Treat and React to Cryptocurrency 72

The Future of Cryptocurrency 76

Benefits and Disadvantages of Cryptocurrency 79

Legal Concern for Cryptocurrency 83

How Big Will Cryptocurrency Impact the World Economy and Which Industries 86

Ways to Store and Really Secure Cryptocurrency 89

When Choosing A Platform; Choose Rapport and Safety First 92

Processes of Cryptocurrency Such As Mining, Wallet, Technology, Blockchain, Smart Contracts, Etc. 94

Ways To Gain And Obtain A Bitcoin 96

Cryptocurrency Is Finance For The Future 99

Big Banks Will Always Dictate 101

Mindset 104

Emerging Markets 113

Cryptocurrency Jobs In The Tech Sector 116

Digital Coins Advance... 119

There Is Always A Dark Side When It The
Crypto Craze 122

Check Your Credit Score Often 126

North Korea and The Hacking Trend............... 129

Crypto Criminals 132

Do Not Forget Your Password........................... 134

Conclusion 138

What Is Cryptocurrency and How Does It Work?

With controlled banks and charges, cryptocurrency takes the third-party and centralized aspect out of the banking world. Think, peer-to-peer, decentralized, and encrypted transactions. Zero banks and government organizations are involved, this is the enticing era of cryptocurrency. As we all know, at the end of the day, we are all controlled by 'the man,' a.k.a 'big banking conglomerates. We sign-up for mortgages, get financed and approved to do so by the bank, this gives banks and the government ultimate power at the end of the day.

Why wouldn't cryptocurrencies be enticing to investors looking to make a real increase in their bank accounts? The digital money era is not controlled by the 'big man banks', cryptocurrency is anonymous, encrypted and electric; cryptocurrency will change the entire globe, once people all over the world start to accept the fact that it works.

The reason why cryptocurrency is taking off is that people want to be in control of their finances. Now we can escape being controlled by banks—the large conglomerates who control everyone. Here in the year 2017, who would have thought that cryptocurrency would take off? Bitcoin is currently at $16K and moving onward and upward. Don't bypass the fact that in December of 2017, Bitcoin's price teeters between $11K and $17K; yes that's quite the jump, a $5K difference. Cryptocurrencies are very exciting for investors who prefer a huge reward. All investors need to be able to stomach a large loss on down days, it is just a reality. If you have a weak stomach, you are better off sticking with traditional stocks, bonds, and options.

Nowadays banks are the middle-man, but the future is meant for the people. With cryptocurrency, people are in charge of their own money, there is no middle-man, as the valued currency is decentralized. This means that the currency is completely digital and can be easily be transferred to others with zero borders.

The way this works, is off of blockchain technology, a public ledger. Whenever a cryptocurrency owner buys, either, Bitcoin, Litecoin, or Eutherum, they can store their currency in an online or offline secure wallet. We recommend that you also give yourself the opportunity to store your valued currency in an offline wallet—for your protection and to prevent fraudulent activity. With crypto-currency, your real name does not have to be displayed.

The goal of cryptocurrency shouldn't necessarily focus on the price itself, as this undermines the true value in what this type of currency aims to do. Basically, cryptocurrency aims to exclude the middle-man and enables people to transfer money anywhere in the world, this concept alone is valuable. With cryptocurrency, people can transfer money from the United States all the way to Venezuela. As you may have heard on the news, Venezuela has run out of cash, because their government was corrupt and made poor choices. This country could certainly benefit from this type of currency—if their government doesn't try to hack them for it.

If you are an avid news reader, you'll learn that Venezuela and their financial market has gone down the drain, literally; it is the year 2017. Grocery costs have surged 100%, if not higher in Venezuela. The people are suffering and decentralizing funds puts the money into the valued owner's hands, as it should be. In our honest speculative opinion, having a currency that can be used worldwide is the safest alternative for the people. There are more pros than cons when it comes to cryptocurrency.

People have been skeptical about the cryptocurrency world, due to the fact that they are simply fearful of getting hacked and their money/currency drowning into the online black abyss of hackers; of course, this is a plausible concern.

But with cryptocurrency platforms ramping up their websites for ongoing security and protection, people who join these reputable exchange platforms should soon feel a peace of mind, as these companies have started to gain plenty of profit to be able to ramp up the support it needs.

The way it works, you buy Bitcoin or Litecoin, whichever currency you decide on, you buy it at current value, after that, you hold short or long-term, this process is similar to stocks, the value can either go up or down, it depends on the worldwide market.

Using *Coinbase* that was founded in 2012, in San Francisco creates more ease and efficiency when it comes to purchasing cryptocurrency on a U.S. exchange. People used to shun this type of currency due to the fact that many thought it was illegal. What people need to realize is that this currency is not illegal, but it has been known to be used for illegal activities. People on the black market, in the very beginning, and perhaps as we speak, have used cryptocurrency to buy illegal drugs on the market. Buying illegal goods on the internet, by transferring cryptocurrency is illegal—remember that.

Now, if you use the currency for legal activities, the currency is not illegal. Use cryptocurrency the proper way, and there shall be no repercussions, it is that simple.

In our honest opinion, we do think that banking moguls write bad media about cryptocurrency because they are scared of going out of business. We don't necessarily need a third-party vendor all of the time. Of course, we are not bashing banks, because let's get real, if your bank funds go missing, the bank will have to step in and investigate, all while refunding you the money that is rightfully yours. Cryptocurrency doesn't have this type of luxury.

We aren't saying banks are going out of business, but what we are saying is that banks will have some competition, either they get with the program or get out! Digital currency is now a hot commodity, it's true, after all, who uses checks these days?

Okay, so you are entirely new to the topic of cryptocurrency, so the word blockchain already went right past your head? This is common, you are new, and we are not expecting you to be a trained enthusiast just yet.

When we say blockchain, we are talking about technology. With the advent of technology, blockchain technology software exists. It is a type of algorithm that is mined by algorithm geniuses at the end of a technological chain who verify transactions that have taken place. An experienced miner can gain valuable Bitcoins or alt coins when they are mining them, same goes for Litecoins. Litecoin is known to have quicker transfer time than Bitcoin. Ethereum is also known to process a lot faster than Bitcoin. It can take up to two minutes to process Ethereum, while it can take up to an hour to fully process Bitcoin [1].

Mining may seem like a hard concept, which in fact it is. Bitcoin mining takes a special type of technical software knowledge to work. If you are not a software tech type of person, then you will have a hard time mining. What we will say, is that mining Bitcoins takes a lot of computer energy, which in turn could get pricey. Power equals money, in the sense of electricity.

---

[1] https://www.thesun.co.uk/money/5127849/ripple-price-xrp-cryptocurrency-spike-buy/

If you want to become a miner, be sure to read our guide to mining cryptocurrency in our next book. We will gladly explain the computer tools you will have to buy and build in order to make cryptocurrency mining a reality.

Coin Lovers

There are plenty of coin lovers out there who stay up-to-date with all the latest coin news. When it comes to coins, collectors usually think of coins as a tangible item. You can sign onto eBay, type in coins, and you will notice that people are selling coins that can range from $1 dollar to hundreds of thousands of dollars. If you happen to be a coin collector, then you need to start taking notice of the cryptocurrency market, these are coins too, just in digital format. People who are up on news have a greater advantage than people who read zero news. You need to learn that the news can help you leverage your financial decisions. Let's face the truth, people who do not invest, grow very little funds over the years, they also face a slow growth, which cannot be recovered in later years. If you really want to be wealthy one day, then we highly suggest that you start looking at digital coins with different eyes. Coins these days, are not completely tangible. The digital currency can be seen with a naked eye on the computer screen, the numbers will be on the screen and you will hold ownership of the digital coin, but you need to remember that when it comes to cryptocurrency you cannot physically hold it, you must do various transfers before you can turn digital into USD or any type of other foreign currency.

Being a trend seeker and researcher will enable an investor to see what is going on in the market early on. Knowing what the next craze is will only create more wealth for the person who is an early seeker. The old saying always stands true, the early bird catches the worm. This phrase is correct, as Bitcoin owners who bought low are the first ones indulging, celebrating, and eating their catch—thousands or millions of dollars.

In our opinion, digital currency is a little safer than penny stocks, as digital currency is not entirely full of a bunch of scam artists, of course, there is another group to worry about—online hackers, but if you have the proper security measures installed and set in place than you don't have anything to worry about for the most part. There are cryptocurrency scam artists, you just need to be aware of what to look out for. Never ever check your cryptocurrency wallet on an unknown Wifi network! Avoid strange emails, and the list goes on, we will explain more shortly.

If you have ever dabbled in penny stocks, then you should know that your risks are entirely abundant, perhaps even more so than cryptocurrency—our opinion.

When it comes to cryptocurrency, you have a choice, to buy into what the crowd has bought, or you can decide to accept cryptocurrency for a means of payment, but either way, you will need a digital wallet to store your new currency in.

Mining is a complicated task and takes a lot of energy, time, and money.

The Blockchain Bubble

The blockchain helps transfer value. Basically, the blockchain is the software that keeps all transactions in order and on a public ledger, verifying each purchase of digital assets going in and out. The blockchain can help with transferring payments across borders. Of course, many people who are critics of the blockchain and cryptocurrency think that the currency is currently in a bubble, which can be entirely true, but no one knows when the bubble is going to pop! There are many speculations, but as with currency and assets, nothing is set in stone as evolution constantly changes depending on the state of the world's economy.

Every new day brings in different challenges and changes. So far, the digital currency has been good to owners of the coin. No one knew Bitcoin was going to blow up to almost $20K, had they knew it would explode exponentially, many people would have bought at low and sold high. In December of 2017, it may be wise to hold onto your Bitcoin's as the digital coin has the ability to grow even higher. Sure, a bubble is possible, almost like the real estate and stock market crash in 2008, so it is best to use your own personal judgment by taking technicals and fundamentals into consideration. Who knows, one day your Bitcoin could be worth a million dollars, anything is posisble. No one wants to be the person who sells their Bitcoin at $20K when it reaches $1M, this will not only be devastating, but very unfortunate. Don't be the person to break this type of news to your future generations, as this dinner talk can lead to guilt and anger. Learning to invest in new ideas early on will help you make headway in life, without having to continually experience the rat race, and never advancing.

Our key advice to take away here is to keep updated with the news every single day. If you really want to advance into newer financial brackets, than we suggest that you don't quit your day job. You do need a steady stream of income to pay your normal bills and you also need investment income that you are not scared to lose, as with any investment—you never really know. There is no insurance for the cryptocurrency world, so we highly suggest that you join a reputable exchange platform like *Coinbase*. When we join reputable and credible companies, they help protect you from future crooks, a.k.a hackers in this case.

Keep in mind, if you invest in a coin that is not well-known and the value is very low, you could risk losing all of your money or you could be considered a lucky person—if the new currencies values hit the sky. This is why we highly suggest if you want to make money off of cryptocurrency than you immerse yourself in the world of digital currency. If you put an hour aside each day to delve into the new currency, this will prove to be beneficial overall.

The people who bought into Bitcoin when the gold coin was under $1K really struck it rich. So you may start to ask yourself, how can you become rich; if you want to strike it rich today, as in December 2017, then you must start looking for a digital currency that has the capability to rise.

Think of possibly investing in ripple, XRP. Ripple is very cheap, the low cost makes Ripple very appealing to investors that want to spend a little and win big. On December 15, 2017, it has been noted on The Sun, that Ripple spiked to 0.8051, which was 46 cents higher per Ripple coin.

There seems to be a lasting trend in 2017, the trend is, as long as Bitcoin keeps growing, other cryptocurrencies also become more valuable as the concept becomes more accepted all around the globe. Once the circulated coins are out and swept up by investors, the value increases. Once this happens, the public will have to look for another likeminded currency, which has to ability to raise too. There are always other trains to catch in the crypto world, it is all about getting on the train at the right exact time, otherwise, you will see a loss. Time is of the essence here.

There is recent news that Amex is now partnering with Ripple in 2017, according to The Sun [2]. Since this is the case, speculators should know that this digital currency will soon have the tools it needs to succeed. It has never been so easy to move money around the globe until cryptocurrencies came into the picture. Now, traders can send, buy, or use their digital currency for anything legal. Just remember, whatever service or product you buy that is in the legal market, you will have to let your CPA know

---

[2] https://www.thesun.co.uk/money/5127849/ripple-price-xrp-cryptocurrency-spike-buy/

your losses and gains for tax purposes at the end of each year; in the U.S. this date in April 15th.

Now that you are aware of how cheap Ripple is, you may want to trade in some of your Bitcoin's to buy Ripple, because this is the only way you can purchase Ripple, you need to acquire and be in possession of Bitcoin to even think of buying this new cryptocurrency. Ripple is not currently on the *Coinbase* exchange, but the platform may decide to adopt Ripple, as in 2018, the currency is set to skyrocket into the future, especially with all of the innovative companies that are seeking to either partner and or adopt payments through digital currency. These type of actions create more value for investors. Ripple has a bullish sign in the ending months of 2017 and into the future of digital currency.

Population Equals Billions!

We all know that China is the most populous nation in the world. Once more and more markets hit the bandwagon, then consider cryptocurrency as high as the sky, really the sky is not the limit with this market, due to scarcity.

The good news here is that, China might be shunning Bitcoin with their government, by banning the currency, but that does not mean cryptocurrency is completely out of the picture in the extremely populous nation, all it means is that China has decided to participate in competitor alternative coins, this is a given, and knowing this fact, we can begin to theorize how large this market will be. Of course, the cryptocurrency market is set to hit into the billions and some have, it really should be no surprise.

Instead, China has decided to invest in OneCoin, a similar type of currency, due to the fact it is run off of blockchain technology. It is a speculative view that China wants to overrule and exceed the almighty Bitcoin that is already worth close to $20K American dollars. Granted there is controversy about OneCoin, but it still is a cryptocurrency, and the public needs to treat it like the digital currency that it is.

There are many traditional investment traders who also shun cryptocurrency, this is fine because as time progresses, they will start to realize that most currency and the way it is run, is off of blockchain technology.

Billions of people wanting in, into the world of cryptocurrency will be the ultimate upside for digital money, which is already proving to be a fact with the current value here in the year 2017. We've recently heard about 'Bitcoin this,' 'Bitcoin that,' this new digital currency is making headlines almost every hour of the day and we highly doubt that this trend will come to a halt.

Top Cryptocurrency To Buy In 2017

Top digital currency to buy at this particular time is Bitcoin and Litecoin. In the last year, Bitcoin has managed to surge 2,000%+, and Litecoin is up almost 5,000%. These currencies are only growing with time and patience. As time progresses into the future, people will start to want a peer-based money market, and that is exactly what cryptocurrency is, taking the government and banks out of the picture, and giving the people more power through advanced software and technology.

We will begin to elaborate in-depth about cryptocurrency and just how valuable this type of currency will get as we move into the future. The future is digital. Of course, there are many other digital currencies that are on the market, we chose these two because their numbers are extraordinary and people have gained plenty of profits thus far. It is the very beginning to a cryptocurrency era. It is important to follow second by second updates when it comes to digital money, as the concept is fairly new and anything can change at the drop of a hat. We highly recommend that you also follow Twitter and the digital currencies that you are aiming to invest in. Following social media sites like Twitter will help you gain insight from other people who have invested in the currency, but use this site wisely, and don't believe everything you read, as there are plenty of people looking to scam this new industry.

The owner of Litecoin, named Charlie Lee is often seen posting on the social medium— Twitter. It is a surprise how much insight one can obtain from glancing and researching this social media site now and then. Bitcoin may be too high to invest in at the moment, but that is why it might be a smart idea to look into something with a similar concept and a similar name. For people looking for a cheaper and underpriced digital currency, the answer is certainly— Litecoin.

If you are in the middle of Litecoin and Bitcoin, another digital currency to invest in is Ethereum. At the time of writing, ETH is worth $477.00. Taking these facts into deep consideration, and using an extremely analytical approach, one can notice that there is one major difference between all of these digital currencies, the one major contrast is that Ethereum, does not have the word coin at the end of the digital brand.

Notice how Bitcoin, Litecoin, and China's new Onecoin all have one thing in common? Yes, that is correct—the word 'coin'. In our speculative opinion, we see the currencies that end in the word 'coin' prevail over the rest of the bunch. Soon we will mention another cryptocurrency that is taking off—IOT (Internet of Things), we will expand upon later in the text below.

If you happen to be in the China market, keep in mind that Bitcoin is banned from China's government; if this applies to you, be sure to research and read about OneCoin, this way you can stay legal with all of your investments. Consistently read the news, as politics change often, which in turn means that each policy has the ability to change when new individuals reign in office and in power.

Professional Platforms To Exchange Cryptocurrency and How They Work

Professional platforms work by providing a secure way to trade digital currency, it is pretty much the same concept as stocks, bonds, and options, although we are dealing with cryptocurrency here—digital money that can be traded and used almost anywhere in the world, that is the whole notion; in a technical sense.

Instead of a centralized bank and government controlling the funds, the platform is used to expedite and enable the process of buying digital money. So in a way, there still is a third-party intervening, well in this case overlooking the process of buying valuable cryptocurrency.

In times of uncertainty, global climate change, financial futures, it is always a good idea to look outside of the box. When you look outside the box, you can see that other avenues really do work. We recommend joining the cryptocurrency team, simply because innovation and advancement always create more wealth. The San Francisco company, named *Coinbase*, is a safe and efficient platform that allows people to buy and sell Bitcoins, Litecoins, and Ethereum, they recently just added Bitcoin Cash to their exchange.

Coinbase competitors include Blockchain and Xapo. These platforms act as a wallet for the cryptocurrency exchange market.

When it comes to *Coinbase*, users funds are insured to an extent, (make sure to read the small and fine print in their privacy disclosure), the company is based in the United States, so if you are from the U.S. it may seem more legitimate to go through this type of platform to sell and to buy your digital currencies.

The year of 2017 has created an all-time high for Bitcoin. The digital currency is rising by the thousands every single day. Sure, we are currently on an upward climb in December 2017, but this doesn't mean the currency isn't volatile. In fact, cryptocurrency is so volatile, which is why people don't want to get involved, they are fearful that Bitcoin is currently at its ultimate high and will abruptly drop. Sure, this can be the case, but if you are an optimist on the other hand, then chances are, you'll believe this cryptocurrency could, in fact, reach the millions on the day. Yes, one Bitcoin could reach the millions if the demand and value are there.

When To Buy and When To Sell Cryptocurrency?

If you are reading this book, and you are a financial guru, then we all should know when to buy and when to sell. We need to sell when the currency is at an all-time high unless we are in it for the long run.

Before you get into this tricky process of selling your cryptocurrency, you first need to decide what kind of investor you are, are you a trend investor, a swing trader, or a long-term type of buyer? You need to decide your type, this way you can stick to a plan and think logically before you make any rash decisions.

When the price is soaring and you begin to start thinking illogically, because all you have on your mind is profit, you need to hold it right there! Stop yourself from panic selling, and think long and hard about the foundation in which you began with. What type of trader are you? Ask yourself this question. These questions will keep you grounded and will help you exit your irrational state of mind. You need every analytical bone in your body if you want to succeed at the game of investments.

Investing is not a game, you are dealing with your hard earned cash; real money that can leave you on a yacht for two, peacefully enjoying life or it can leave you—rotten poor. You have to invest in your future wisely.

Always buy the dip. This ensures that you gain forward momentum if the price doesn't dip any further that is. Keep in mind that cryptocurrencies are not so similar to stocks, as they have plenty of differences. With this in mind, we need to be able to handle incredible highs and lows—this is just the name of the game.

If you happen to be new to investing, we welcome you to a new and exciting world in finance. To make matters easier to understand, buying on the dip is referring to buying at a low price when the price falls during each trade and depending on the market. The great thing about cryptocurrency, is that the market never closes, yes it is open 24/7 around the clock, 365 days a week. Financial gurus have dreamed about this type of trading session, really, who hasn't? Think about digital currency this way—the money never sleeps literally!

Once you invest in cryptocurrency, you have to get used to scenarios like this, one moment you'll log on to your Coinbase account and see that you are up exponentially, the next hour you look, the loss could result in thousands of dollars lost.

We can't give this information out securely, but what we can do, is make a suggestion. Our advice would be to research as much as you can get your hands on. Ebooks like this one are obviously helpful, this way you can learn the in's and out's of cryptocurrency, but we also recommend that you keep up on the daily price moves your digital currency is making.

On the platform, Coinbase, you will be able to analyze charts and see real-time data, this way you can determine what a low buy is and what is too high. No one wants to get trapped into an investment knowing they bought the currency at a valued price that is way too high. Before you decide to purchase this type of currency, learn everything you can, and read the news regarding cryptocurrency every time a new news article is posted. Perhaps set a Google alert on your mobile or laptop device, this way you can be assured that you will not miss any update that is posted. When it comes to investing, you need to know everything you possibly can about the currency in which you are buying, after all, you are dealing with your hard earned cash that you work day in and day out for. Spend your funds wisely, only to create long-term and additional wealth for you, your family, and your future.

The question is, when should you buy cryptocurrency? Well, to figure out this decision, you must first decide how much money you can put aside to invest? Are you looking to invest a couple of hundred of dollars? If this is the case, then you should look at buying Litecoin, if you have tens of thousands to invest, then you may consider investing in Bitcoin, but be careful.

Since the market is still semi new, the outcome for long-term growth is unpredictable. Perhaps sit down, go over your finances, and figure out just how much money you have in your investing budget.

If you are a trend investor, and you have calculated how much money you would like to make, then consider selling once your profits exceed your goal—as a trend investor doesn't hold onto investments too long, and aims only to create short-term profit.

It all depends on your investment habits. Whether you are a long-term investor or a short-term swing trader, you need to do what works for you and your monetary budget.

We must chime in at this moment, if you were lucky enough to buy your cryptocurrency at its all-time low then consider yourself blessed. Be grateful, as we highly advise holding for the long-term. Currencies such as Bitcoin have been compared to gold, so if you want to see the extravagant outcome in years to come, it may be wise to watch, wait, and see your digital money rise without lifting a finger.

What Kinds of Currencies Are Counting As Cryptocurrency, Which One Have Biggest Impact Such As Bitcoin, etc.?

Everyone knows Bitcoin, it has been hitting the news headlines left and right, how could we miss it? There is often talk about Bitcoin in the films, and television shows that we watch. It wasn't until the platform Coinbase opened that people of the general public were able to finally feel comfortable buying cryptocurrency. Sure the San Francisco company, Coinbase, allows an easier trading process, but Bitcoin has been around long before Coinbase was able to offer a safe investing platform.

Billionaires and millionaires already had insider information and were already in-the-know. They had first dibs and knew this type of currency was going to be a hit, hence why they were the first ones to invest and gain. It wasn't a huge surprise, but to Warren Buffet who wasn't a big fan of the currency, it was, and he—missed out.

Keep in mind, just because Bitcoin is at an all-time high, this doesn't mean that it is the best cryptocurrency to buy. There are other digital currencies on the market of course, which have the ability to be much more lucrative for the everyday investor.

Although, there have been some analysts who think Bitcoin could reach as high as $100K, don't bank on their knowledge, and speculate for yourself; this advice is key.

Litecoin is very similar to Bitcoin, in fact, it is a good choice if you are wanting to get into the cryptocurrency market and planning to not break your bank. Bitcoin is at such a high price, don't fall into the bubble; if it's too high, don't bother.

Remember buying at the lowest price is always the best decision when picking up any new investment. No one wants to be the one left 'holding the bag'.

Litecoin is an interesting currency because it is so similar to Bitcoin and is relatively cheap at the moment here in December 2017. Once all 84 million Litecoins have circulated, the value will certainly rise high as the demand will go up. People who are holding at a low buy-in are the winners in this sense. Unlike Bitcoin, Litecoin was created by a former Google Engineer named Charles Lee. The currency came to fruition in 2011, while Bitcoin was made in 2009. Both digital currencies are not even a decade old, hence why they have skyrocketing futuristic potential.

Bitcoin and Litecoin share different algorithms. The main purpose of Litecoin was to make something similar to Bitcoin, but new and improved. It takes longer to mine Bitcoin, around ten minutes, while it can take around two and half minutes to mine Litecoin. Litecoin is much more efficient and faster than Bitcoin.

How To Minimize Risks With Trading and Investing Cryptocurrency

Minimize your risks by placing your assets elsewhere. As we've mentioned several times, you can't put all of your eggs in one basket, unless you are a complete basket case. Although, some basket cases have made it out more than alive and with millions upon millions of dollars. Sure there are cases like this, but the chances aren't that high. To minimize risk when it comes to trading and investing, we urge investors to stay up-to-date on the latest developments day in and day out. Read the current events and news that relate to cryptocurrency and read about the exchange platform companies. Keep an eye on your assets and don't entirely forget about them as you do when you invest in a company like

Apple Inc. You are dealing with real dollars, so it is imperative that you stay keen to effectively manage your assets; no one else will do it for you.

Have an emergency savings stash, invest in stocks and bonds, keep working at the job you love, even when you do hit the million dollar mark—it will keep your brain healthy and fresh, also, make sure to buy real estate and increase your equity by remodeling your home or buying in an area that will be going up on the market; diligent research is everything when it comes to minimizing all potential risks.

As with any investing, it is important to look at the fundamentals and technical analysis when trying to determine your short and long-term outlooks.

Start with reading the news, learn everything and anything, and learn to calculate the technical charts. When breaking down technical analysis, you need to start by looking at charts, if you have the appropriate software, then you should compare and analyze charts with precision.

Mistakes To Avoid When Trading and Investing Cryptocurrency For Beginners And Advanced

There are plenty of mistakes that beginners can learn to avoid before they are caught up in the cryptocurrency rush. One key factor is not to get caught up in the mainstream media and news and buy at an all-time high.

Investors need to strategically study the price, second by second, to get the best price. The whole idea is to buy low, sell high. Digital currency investment is similar to stock investments in this sense. At this point, we can always speculate what is high, but we are not quite there yet. This is another reason why we don't necessarily recommend that investors sell when Bitcoin is at a high of a $17K. The currency has a ton of potential that might be beyond what anyone can speculate at this particular moment in time.

Advanced investors, don't sell your Bitcoin's, you might want to wait until all 21 million Bitcoin's have circulated, perhaps your currency value will be greater than you thought it could be. Don't be hasty when it comes to Bitcoin, as many have speculated that the digital currency, could be a bubble waiting to pop. Sure, pessimists are likely to follow this kind of thought process, but in the end, we all know that investments go up and down. This type of investment is an investment worth waiting for.

15 Effective Strategies or Effective Ways To Make Money With Cryptocurrency and Become A Millionaire

1. Pay off all debt

If you want to start investing, you need first to stop accumulating interest fees that are adding to your debt. Pay every company off first and foremost. Stop compiling more debt, get rid of it, before you start making any major investments. Gain a reality check; this is the only way you will succeed and get ahead.

2. Have an emergency savings account

Life is precarious; we never know what new days will bring us. This is why it is imperative to have savings for unexpected emergencies that may arise.

3. Buy low

As we have been reiterating, you must buy low in order to succeed in achieving investment profits. The same question always arises, what exactly is buying low? To buy investments low, you need to figure out a time to buy at a particular drop. The right timing is all it takes when it comes to buying low. Research for as long as you have to, or purchase technical software, this way you are enabled to choose to buy the currency at the lowest rate it is selling for, once you do this, it will be hard to lose.

4. Research, strategize, and plan

It is important to strategically plan finances and investments appropriately. An investor needs to be organized and needs to have the ability to plan for the future.

5. Calculate technical analysis

Calculating technical analysis can be done through reading charts and analyzing them by day, hour, minute by minute, or by the second.

Technical charts are very complicated to read if you are not an expert. We do recommend that you research financial charts in-depth in order to strategically prevail with this method.

6. Stay updated with fundamental knowledge
When we say fundamental, if you are already a stock investor then this word should not seem like a surprise to you. When a fundamental analysis is taking place, the investor needs to look at all aspects related to the business, whether it is related to financials, CEO breaking news, changes in the organization, sell offs, buy-ins, competitors, etc. The list of fundamentals is long, but all of these scenarios and business matters need to be properly analyzed to properly make a calculated and more sound financial decision regarding a cryptocurrency investment.

7. Read cryptocurrency news
As you know, the digital currency market is entirely volatile, one day Bitcoin could be worth $17K USD, and on another day, even hours later,

the price can plummet to $9K USD, it all really depends on the market and what the public wants.

8. Spread your investments around

Don't spend all of your money on cryptocurrency, it is important to save finances for everyday expenses along with saving for a rainy day when the finances are crucially needed. Once you have these safety nets, you can then begin to invest in several assets. You need to keep in mind that assets are not liabilities and they provide a way to make more money; profit. Think of it this way, if you purchase a car, you are basically buying a liability. Once you walk off of the car lot, the value of the car will go down, due to the fact that a numerous of liabilities can happen to the car—it can gain a dent, become totaled, with mileage, the cars value goes down, etc. On the contrary, if you buy a house, it is considered more of an asset as it will gain in equity and value—most of the time. Cryptocurrencies are only valuable once they gain value. But as we keep reiterating, these type of currencies are new, so their volatility is tremendously high. This is why, we highly encourage people to diversify their investments, in hopes to balance out all assets and liabilities.

9. Protect your assets

We can't mention it enough times in this book. You buy crypto, you need to protect your assets. Otherwise they can get stolen, hacked, or lost. There will be no big bank to bail you out, you are on your own in this realm. Security is utmost important in the technology age.

10. Keep passwords offline

Once you read further, you will find various strategies that you can utilize to keep your assets safe—follow them and don't be lazy as laziness can cost you thousands and thousands of dollars. Your mind must stay keen in order to stay up with this new world of finance. It is also important to have knowledge about the technology sector, after all, this currency would not exist, if you had not moved into a tech era.

11. Don't focus solely on Bitcoin

Bitcoin may be in the limelight now, but this will not always be the case. We do mention throughout this book, what new emerging coins might be worth a look. Hint* Look for coins that are a deal of a lifetime and are soon-to-be partnering with large corporations. This is a sign that something good is cooking. Keep up-to-date on all cryptocurrency, rather than just Bitcoin. So what if Bitcoin hits a million, there are other coins that will follow shortly after the Bitcoin king. Pay close attention to these if you do not own any Bitcoin and can't afford it at its current price.

12. Find low alternate coins

IOTA and Ripple are good examples of alternate coins that have the ability to grow into the future as other cryptocurrency gains news attention and public validity.

13. Become a trend investor

Being a trend investor might be satisfying for people who love excitement. If you happen to get get a thrill when it comes to crypto and when it comes to trends, than consider yourself hit with a double whammy. If you decide to become this type of investor, you need to make sure that you buy when something is low and hot, and sell when it is over valued, but still hot. You will be moving extremely fast if this is the trading route you decide to take in the cryptocurrency world.

14. Be a swing trader

A swing trader is just a bit different than trend investors. These type of traders, basically trade on the swing. A good example, say Bitcoin is going for $9K, the investor buys in at $9K and pays the *Coinbase* exchange fees, estimate $9,100.00, perhaps less. The day moves on and Bitcoin moves up to $14K, the swing trader will most likely sell, so they can make the profit in the gap of $9,100-$14K, making a total of $5K. For swing traders, this is a rinse and repeat type of strategy, it can be very lucrative.

15. Invest for the Long-term

If you are a long-term investor, than you don't have to look at your wallet often. Basically long-term investors are in it for the long haul, so why wait and watch the paint dry? We'd rather go about our life and look at our accounts every now and then. This will ease the stress of seeing such highs and lows when it comes to the hard earned dollars that we watch.

Once you get past the newbie stage, you'll begin to learn what type of investment strategy works for you. It takes time, in fact, everything good in life always takes time.

The Terminologies Related To Cryptocurrency

There are many different terminologies when it comes to cryptocurrency. Let's start with Coinbase, a reputable cryptocurrency trading platform that allows investors to trade, Bitcoin, Litecoin, or Ethereum, and now Bitcoin Cash. The platform provides an online wallet; you can enter your dashboard, buy and sell, have access to your accounts, tools, and settings options—navigate through these buttons and manage the credit card or ACH account and routing number that is attached. Once the investor deposits money into an online Coinbase wallet, the investor can then delete their credit card information if he or she chooses too as an extra measure of safety. Of course, this is not recommended if the investor plans to deposit or withdrawal money into their <u>Coinbase</u> often.

Digital money around the globe, similar to a one world currency, never sleeps. The digital currency can be bought with different forms of currency, such as the American dollar or a Rupee. Once the currency is bought, transactions can be done anywhere in the world with zero fees. Although, the buyer and seller do have fees, and these fees are looked at as trading and platform fees. Simply put, the fees are relatively low, compared to the gains investors will see on their return.

Mining-A process of using technology and electrical power, along with algorithms, and the proper mathematical knowledge to solve a technology algorithm on the public ledger. Some Software Engineers can mine Bitcoins, in return creating value and profit for themselves; earning themselves cryptocurrency coins.

Dip-When the technical data and price fall from a previous monetary high.

Bitcoin-The creator is named, Satoshi Nakamoto, he started out by distributing an accounting ledger, which is named the blockchain, he enabled this so people can take units of value, meaning they don't need to trust a centralized authority; a bank.

Litecoin-The creator of this crypto coin is Charlie Lee, he is a software engineer and formerly worked for *Google* in this position. He founded Litecoin the digital currency in 2013.

Onecoin- Software Developers in China created Onecoin, but there is a rumor that this digital currency falls under the scheme category. When investing in cryptocurrency, you always want to buy branded reputable and credible names over coins you have not heard much about.

Cryptocurrency Platforms- Coinbase, Binance, Bittrex, Kraken, Bitfinex, Coinmania, LocalBitcoins, Gemini, Bitstamp, CEX.IO, and Busque; Coinbase, is our first choice.

How Government and Financial Services Treat and React to Cryptocurrency

Here is a little curveball, why don't government and financial services treat cryptocurrency with glamour and glory? Well, for one it is decentralized, meaning it is not controlled by them, it is controlled by blockchain technology which provides a public ledger through software technology that records in the blockchain who bought what and for how much, in real-time.

Blockchain technology provides a more secure way to keep records, think of a public ledger being documented at the very moment the transaction took place. Miners are used to verifying each transaction, all while collecting a coin for the energy and intellectual mathematical algorithms that they solve.

Banks are not too fond of this new type of currency, simply because they have lost all control, or they may think they've lost control, but this is only the beginning. Digital currency looks to put the control notion back into the investor's hands, not the banks or the governments. So, of course, these types of organizations are going to shun this newer type of cryptocurrency. When the government and banks lose control, either they try to outlaw it or condemn it. Once they do this, perhaps they will gain control by allowing all of their institutions to buy in first, hence placing the power back into their hands anyway. In 2018, banks will most likely try to regulate this currency, due to the large sums of money investors have received. This type of currency might just be a trend that lasts. There's plenty of smart investors getting ready to give crypto a go.

Although keep in mind, with technology advancing every day, blockchain technology is more secure than not, because once an investor or buyer purchases this type of currency, it is immediately logged into the public ledger, which cannot be denied or erased.

Some financial services are realizing the potential when it comes to cryptocurrency, so of course, Wall Street investors are jumping all over Bitcoin. It did raise from a high $9K dollars to $17K in a matter of weeks.

Let's all keep in mind, that there are plenty of naysayers, when it comes to this type of currency, after all, December 11, 2017, *Coinbase*, the platform's site went down very briefly, although this issue was resolved, shortly after. Forbes online publication has recognized that *Coinbase* is actually adding over 100K users a day [3]! These

---

3

https://www.forbes.com/sites/jessedamiani/2017/12/19/crypto-watch-verge-xvg-price-climbs-800-in-a-type of financial platforms aren't necessarily amped up like NASDAQ or the New York Stock Exchange, although, Bitcoin's CEO did make a statement that, "We have increased the size of our support team by 640% and launched phone support in September"—according to the *Business Insider*[4]. During the afternoon scare during this scenario, Bitcoin or Litecoin did not see any plummet. In fact, the currencies began to steadily rise.

From this instance alone, we can then make a statement, as long as cryptocurrency exchange platforms stay on top of their website infrastructure and security, this industry will continue to grow into the billions, this is what smart investors speculate.

---

week-what-is-xvg-and-why-is-it-growing-so-fast/#18b08ffd444e
[4] http://www.businessinsider.com/coinbases-cryptocurrency-exchange-crashes-briefly-2017-12

The Future of Cryptocurrency

The future of cryptocurrency in December of 2017 looks very positive, although some analysts may state that the future remains very volatile. Although, climate enthusiasts can argue, that too much energy is used to mine Bitcoin's and likeminded digital currency, because mining uses quite a tremendous amount of energy on an annual basis.

Cryptocurrency is the future. Think about it, what are you most likely going to buy your children and family members for the holidays and their birthdays? Sure you can get them clothing, and small gifts, but if you really want to impress and reward your family members, then you'd better get them their favorite technological device. The latest Apple gadgets are always a hit, and you only live once, right? Just think about all of the technology that you use on a daily basis, it is practically embedded into us at this point, we forget that we use it so often.

Once we move past the cryptocurrency talk, which won't happen since this book is the foundational beginning for anyone looking to learn about digital money, we can then move into IOTA (internet of things). There are plenty of people who are confused when it comes to buying cryptocurrency in the 'internet of things'. In this guide to cryptocurrency, we will simplify everything for you, as Bitcoins can be used to buy IOTA.

Joining *Binance* enables investors to buy IOTA at a low price with their digital currency. IOTA is set to explode in the year 2018 since the mainstream population is starting to catch the latest and hottest news regarding Bitcoin.

So again, if you are asking if there is going to be a future for Bitcoin and Litecoin, the answer is yes. These digital currencies are hot on the market now, but the vast space of the internet and technology has no limit. Exciting? Sure.

Picture this, since IOTA can only be bought with digital currency, what is the message here? The message is simple, there will be more avenues to spend your cryptocurrency and gain value for yourself. Yes, it is possible to be a new investor and become a self-made millionaire with smart money habits, this is a large possibility, especially if the investor decides to get in, early on.

Benefits and Disadvantages of Cryptocurrency

The pros and cons range vastly, of course. The pros are that Bitcoin is turning mainstream and the 21 million Bitcoins that are currently circulating, won't be around for long—this idea certainly brings up the value. Downsides? Well, cryptocurrency investments and industries are extremely volatile as it is still very fresh to the market. Warren Buffet did warn against this type of investment, but we have to keep in mind, that he is an investor of the past. Sure he gained his money through investments through companies like Coca-Cola, etc. companies that offered a product, while newer investors are gaining their money off of technology. Time changes and so do hot commodities of the world.

Of course, there is much security scares when it comes to this digital money, because it is new, and is not regulated; this is a valid concern. To succeed at cryptocurrency, you need to be fully aware that you need to stay skeptical and keep your guard up, especially when you are protecting your funds in your online wallet. Apple IOS has reported that there are IOS-based wallets in app stores, but people need to be aware, that there are also fake IOS wallets out there and they need to know about this when they are downloading any new wallet. Always keep up with the latest security news and never trust a company you haven't researched thoroughly, as you could create financial devastation if you don't protect yourself to the maximum.

Also, make sure to never store your platform's exchange password on your computer. Keep matters safe, write it down, and lock it up in your safe that is fireproof.

Of course, any newbie has the right to think that cryptocurrency exchanges are sketchy, because in the beginning, they are, especially if you are not used to the industry. Not knowing puts the investor at a disadvantage. There is an upside to this particular factor, the answer is, truthful blockchain technology.

There are centralized forms of digital currencies, but in December of 2017, there is news and word that technologists are in fact replacing centralized currencies into decentralized; this is brilliant for the people, as the people need to be handed back the torch once again.

Of course, there are many vulnerabilities when it comes to decentralization, but as long as you research the perfect companies, ramp up your security, and invest a modest but good enough amount, then you can limit your risks.

The same goes for everyday life, we walk outside and we never know what we will encounter, but if we didn't go to work, and take a chance, then we would be missing out on living a better life; instead we have created a life that we comfortably made for ourselves with the paycheck we gain every time we go to work. If we don't take calculative risks especially with our finances, then how do we expect to grow?

Life is full of vulnerabilities, in this book, we teach you a plethora of knowledge about cryptocurrencies, this way you can learn to calculate and lower your risk of losing any monetary means while you are in the investing process.

Legal Concern for Cryptocurrency

As mentioned earlier, banks condemn against this type of digital currency. There is plenty of speculation about this action, as they are trying everything in their power not to go bankrupt. Decentralization takes big banks out of the market; think, out of sight and out of mind. Banks and government agencies have tried, time and time again to give a bad reputation to cryptocurrency markets, but in the recent months, nearing the end of the year 2017, cryptocurrencies seem to be thriving, though government and banking agencies spread bad speculation.

As long as you report to your CPA every year, how much you invested and how much profit you've gained and lost, and as long as you don't use the cryptocurrency for illegal activity, you should feel safely guarded. The only way you should feel you have a legal concern, is if you are in fact using your cryptocurrency for illegal activity. The IRS is veering in on the crypto market solely because it has recently hit mainstream and is set to make them billions of dollars in the longer-term, if they catch illegal cryptocurrency holders.

When it comes to legality, it is very important to always stay in-the-know, as this will keep you updated on all legal rules that pertain to this digital currency. You can empower yourself by researching the internet, use it to your advantage and as a tool. Go to *Google,* and type in cryptocurrency legal news, you'll find real-time updated news that will be helpful when it comes to learning the law that surrounds cryptocurrency.

Of course, everyone has a concern about anything and everything, especially nowadays with our personal information being on the internet, in digital form, and being very accessible to people who want to do damage—hackers. You need to make sure that you are secure nevertheless, read about safe cryptocurrency wallets, which we will get into in later chapters. Don't fall for phishing scams, and only use reputable companies that are trusted when buying or purchasing cryptocurrency.

Bitcoin is starting to lose its bad reputation, the rep that is was known for via the dark web; cryptocurrencies are building a sustainable type of name for future finance. The steady climb of Bitcoin has enabled all cryptocurrencies to gain a more reliable momentum and name.

How Big Will Cryptocurrency Impact the World Economy and Which Industries

Of course, this is completely speculative, but with continued research, we can continue to say that our opinion remains positive, as people are looking for ways to have the currency without dealing with a bank, a.k.a—the middle-man. If we can take out the middle man and people can exchange currency all around the globe without any additional fees, then why not? This will always be the question that will remain.

Bitcoin may be extremely volatile, but at the end of the day, so are other currencies in the digital era that exists. These particular cryptocurrencies are not a short-term hold; they are certainly a long-term hold. Perhaps in 20-30 years, a Bitcoin holder will be a valued millionaire, of course, anything is possible? Or perhaps the currency will explode too high and then fall to an absolute bottom? There are many scenarios. We don't suggest that you invest your whole life savings in this type of currency, as it is most important to spread out your investments for maximum long-term gain, but if you have something to invest and your bills are all paid off, and the money is just sitting around collecting dust— then sure, make a smart decision. Always remember to intelligently analyze the daily price moves of whichever currency you are going to buy. Never buy blindly, that is the best advice that we can give.

Cryptocurrency can, in fact, change the world as the currency can be used worldwide, there are no currency changes that need to take place. This means that there is one type of currency that can be used—digital currency. As it is, we sign online, onto our bank accounts and the numbers we see inside of our online accounts are digital, so why wouldn't online digital currency be the next step?

Cryptocurrency will not only affect one industry or market; the idea can, in fact, have the ability to play a domino effect, but not in a bad way. Perhaps one day in the future, digital currency will be known as king? This is kind of far off, but not so much. Of course people like security and computers can be hacked, and with no centralized bank looking after this deregulated currency, large hacking sums of money, and the currency just vanishing, is another possibility. This is why we are not betting our full futures solely on this type of currency, although it is a smart idea to spread out investments.

Let's put it into perspective, people in the future will be able to use cryptocurrency to purchase homes, goods, and services, as long as the digital currency is accepted, it is simply that simple. This example alone is the reason why cryptocurrency will soon dominate the world of finance.

Ways to Store and Really Secure Cryptocurrency

As we already mentioned, *Coinbase* is a trusted platform out of San Francisco, California. We highly recommend that any person who is U.S. based, purchase through this platform as it is the safest way to secure, buy, and sell cryptocurrencies. The platform offers secure wallets for people to store their Bitcoins, Litecoins, Ethereum, or Bitcoin Cash coins in.

All investors who seek to buy and acquire cryptocurrency need to be super aware that there are plenty of criminals out in the market and on the prowl. They are constantly looking to steal online assets that aren't theirs. Keeping your assets secure always needs to be the first priority and on every cryptocurrency investors mind.

Cybercriminals always attack vulnerable prey when it comes to seeking out a target.

There are other exchanges on the market too, such as Binance and plenty of others, which offer online wallets too. To protect yourself, you need to store your assets offline. You can do this by storing your currency on a USB drive, which is also known as cold storage.

As an investor, you should be aware of technology and the operating systems that are involved. With that said, operating systems can lead to leaked information without the user's consent, making it easier for crooks to get into your online wallet. If you want to be the next cryptocurrency millionaire than it is wise that you are aware of the what if's. Because you won't be a millionaire if a hacker tries draining your wallet into their incognito account, simply for reasons you could have avoided had you been more prepared.

Security measures are everything in the world of technology. You must keep updating your security and operating systems, as Developers are constantly changing and upgrading bug fixes and issues on the regular. In our opinion, Apple Inc. is safer than HP, because there is an extra layer of built-in security on Apple computers, thank you Apple!

Since you are looking at making millions of dollars with cryptocurrency, you can start by storing your assets in a hardware wallet titled, *Trezor,* or a cold storage wallet named *Bitkey*, which can strongly protect you from theft. Once you get to the million dollar mark in assets, you will certainly want to take these extra precautions and methods to protect your funds at all costs, it is better you take this precaution early on. In the crypto world, you are responsible for making sure your Bitcoins or other alternative coins are safe.

When Choosing A Platform; Choose Rapport and Safety First

Before you sign-up with a cryptocurrency exchange platform, you need to ask yourself a few questions.

- Is the platforms website secure and safe?

- Can you take your funds out immediately? What is the minimum and maximum you can withdraw at a time?

- What is the transaction fee that the exchange is currently implementing?

- Does the exchange offer a view of real-time prices?

- What is the main 'buying' currency is it USD or Euros?

- What other alternative coins does the exchange offer? (Binance has a lot more options than *Coinbase*, although *Coinbase* just added Bitcoin Cash, this could signal the fact that *Coinbase* is on their way to add more alternative coins to their exchange)

- Is the website user-friendly?

- What are the ratings of the exchange?

- What are the customer reviews?

Depending on what country you are in, try to stick with platforms based in your country, this will make things a lot easier in the long run.

Processes of Cryptocurrency Such As Mining, Wallet, Technology, Blockchain, Smart Contracts, Etc.

Mining Bitcoins and cryptocurrencies requires an intelligent technology software genius to use the right amount of electrical power, which can, in turn, be costly. Mining requires the right algorithms and knowledge, along with plenty of patience. Mining is certainly not easy, but for the people who are experienced in Bitcoin, Litecoin, or other cryptocurrency mining, the outcome is always rewarding. These digital currencies can be obtained through mining.

When it comes to mining cryptocurrencies, intelligent and knowledgeable people and computers have to solve a very difficult 64 digit mathematical solution as with Bitcoin. The mathematical solution is a way for miners to verify transactions that took place; this is used as a solution in the blockchain. Of course, other cryptocurrencies require a different amount of digits.

Ways To Gain And Obtain A Bitcoin

There are plenty of ways to obtain a Bitcoin, as we mentioned earlier, people who are competent enough and can solve complex mathematical algorithms to create the next block on the blockchain can gain Bitcoin's, but it is not as easy as it sounds.

Small companies and businesses can add and accept Bitcoin, Litecoin, or other cryptocurrencies. They will provide a sign for customers to pay for merchandise this way. Whenever there is a sign to accept such goods, and cryptocurrency is an offered way to pay, via a Bitcoin, Litecoin, or whichever cryptocurrency is accepted, a merchant can gain a coin. A lot of newer companies are opening their doors to the cryptocurrency market, which certainly paves way for digital currency success.

There are other ways to gain a Bitcoin, for instance, *Coinbase,* offers $10.00 of Bitcoin to a person who refers a new investor who invests over $100.00 USD into cryptocurrency. So, if you happen to be an ultimate online marketing genius, than we highly recommend that you start sharing your *Coinbase* code to online users, sooner rather than later, hypothetically, if you get 1 million new investors to sign-up with *Coinbase,* and they invest over $100.00 USD dollars, than you could be a new generation of a cryptocurrency millionaire.

We have all heard about the Winklevoss brother's who gained a settlement from Facebook, Mark Zuckerberg. These are the brothers who apparently gave Mark Zuckerberg the original idea to create Facebook; the brothers are also the first known billionaires who profited off of Bitcoin. So yes, you should want to know about how they gained their billion dollar wealth status. From the Facebook settlement they gained $65 million dollars and used around $11 million dollars for their cryptocurrency investment— Bitcoin. They came out way ahead of the game!

These brothers knew that investing in something new and valuable was only going to bring their profits up. At the end of the day, when you log into your bank account, what do you see? Digital numbers, numbers that make up your bank account, we can't stress this fact enough. There have been many of people who have made a lot of money with cryptocurrency, but this is just the beginning when it comes to digital currency, as the currency is encrypted for safety and security, decentralized, and can be used all over the world for trade and has zero fees.

Cryptocurrency Is Finance For The Future

As we can see, there is a lot of media about cryptocurrency, but just because mainstream says to look towards digital currency, this is not a good reason to cash out all of your savings and all of your stock accounts to purchase this type of currency. Although, since this currency is entirely speculative and more and more businesses are offering the option to pay with cryptocurrency, we can begin to state that this currency is going somewhere, especially if large corporations begin to adopt this type of financial transaction. Cryptocurrencies do not have an ebb and flow type of growth, either they shoot up really high, or the sore extremely downward, so if you have a weak heart and stomach, and you are easily stressed out, it is strongly not recommended not to invest a great amount.

Sure, if you are looking to make gains, invest a little here and a little there, and in coming years, perhaps even a decade down the road, you'll be proud you kept up with the latest trends. Be careful though, because trends have been known to die down—once mainstream jumps on board.

Big Banks Will Always Dictate

After a long workday, we come home, check our mail, and some of us will receive a bill to pay our mortgages, because after all, in America, the dream that we have been fed our whole lives is to get an education (even if you have to finance it), get a job, get married, have a child, and buy a house; this is what we have been fed to believe. This is not necessarily the right path to choose, as it is a stable path, it does not always guarantee ultimate success. After all, we still have mortgages and student loans, and when those large sums are all paid off, we still have health and taxes to worry about. Who controls the mortgages? The bank controls them. And who controls healthcare? The government likes to claim they do, but when the day is over, we are paying our high premiums, and the money is going directly to the bank.

Eliminating the bank and decentralizing finance is a new and improved way of thinking. People who opt for this type of finance can be considered the anarchists of finance.

Banks will eventually have to give in when it comes to cryptocurrency. The banks are already doing so. In the year 2018, many top banks will go ahead and invest in cryptocurrency to try and keep their control as discussed.

According to *Coindesk*, big banks will start to buy into cryptocurrencies in the year 2018, in order to increase their foreign reserves[5]. It all makes sense, perhaps the government is trying to scare the public about cryptocurrencies, so they can be the ones to buy-in and disperse the new digital currency as it sees fit? It is the almighty and

---

[5] https://www.coindesk.com/2018-year-central-banks-begin-buying-cryptocurrency/

powerful bank, after all. If the banks know the public is buying into this kind of currency, they too are going to want to own it, in fact, they will want to own all of it if they can. This is another theory about how big banks will try to regulate the currency, so getting in now is worthwhile unless you want to be sitting in the dust.

Mindset

As long as you stay true to yourself, follow your gut and research logic, you can create a financially sound future. You need to make a point, while you are in the new phase of buying cryptocurrency, to envision your success. If you can't see your dream, who can? You need to start by following smart habits. Smart habits include: creating income, paying off debt first, saving for emergencies, creating steady income flow, investing in cryptocurrencies, stocks and bonds, real estate and equity, not going out to eat every single night, living below your means, saving and budgeting for vacations, and the list goes on. Once you are in the proper mindset, you have educated yourself, then go out and buy cryptocurrency on the *Coinbase or Gemini* exchange.

Sure there are some success stories about the tech slacker who invested in Bitcoin and is now a millionaire, we certainly don't doubt it. This could be your success story too if you just let it happen. Envision your future and how much profit you will gain. Start to set a goal, now type up that goal, print it, and frame it. Place this monetary goal somewhere you see every morning you wake up. When you see a goal and reminder every morning, it will be visible, and more tangible. You will soon see that after looking at your goal day in and day out, that it will slowly come to a reality. For cryptocurrencies sake, your goal could arrive a lot faster. As mentioned, the digital currency sees large gaps of highs and lows, the currency moves quicker than the snail-like stock market. Cryptocurrency is for the movers and the shakers who can spare anywhere from $1K-$10K USD. The middle-class may soon be able to enter a new class once these currencies gain in value. Perhaps after all of the institutions follow the 99% trend. Trends come and go, but if you look at the uses cryptocurrency has, there is a possibility to stick around. Bubble or no bubble, everyone should get the 'fear of missing out' vibe when it comes to Bitcoin and cryptos in general.

There are many people in the government and financial agencies who are trying to downplay the worldwide use of this one world type of currency, hence why cryptocurrency has been given a notorious reputation. Cryptocurrency is making a huge fuss because not only do the government and big banks know how much money this currency drives, the general population has caught on, and it is the people who are using their dollars to invest in something that could be the beginning of a large financial explosion.

After all, what is the worst that can happen? An economic downfall? It is not like the world has not already gone through this. The middle-class is about to grow into a new financial bracket, well not the ones that did not adopt cryptocurrency early on. As you know, it can go either way, a crypto crash or a crypto craze, it all depends on how you look at it. Don't forget that as soon as something new comes along, the other trend will gain momentum, and the current one can lose momentum, this is just how the market works. If the cryptocurrency that you decided to buy into loses its momentum, before you make a rash decision and sell low, start to think that there are other days where you have witnessed extreme highs. If you are that worried about your money then it is wise to set a percentage loss for yourself. This will help you decide when to sell if the price drops below your percentage loss. For instance, losing 1% of $1K USD, you would see a $100.00 dollar loss and so on.

It is not just about cryptocurrency, it is about the blockchain solution, embed this into your brain. The solution is not some large bank overlooking and verifying the funds, the solution is a blockchain in technology that is verified by other currency users. The blockchain numbers cannot be incorrect as each value is stored on a public ledger, eradicating any errors. Let's think back to when Well's Fargo recently made up fake accounts under past and current account holders; in the blockchain solution, this error and fraud simply cannot take place. Cryptocurrency isn't the only digital currency that participates in the blockchain, banks and institutions are finally taking notice as this craze continues.

Perhaps blockchain technology was disregarded as non important in the past? This is always a possibility. The blockchain provides imperative and scientifically notated truth. Of course, skeptics may want to disregard this statement and say that with technology solutions, errors can also occur; this argument is just as valid as the rest of them. Should the recent growth stop you from advancing your future with profit? The answer is up to you. If you have enough to 'throw away' then sure, try investing, but if you are incredibly fearful that your investment will become a big fat zero and it will ruin your life, then we highly suggest that you keep your hard earned dollars in an interest gaining savings account.

Putting all eggs in one basket is never a good move. You must start to think like a Grandmaster at chess. You need to be strategic and know when to move your king (cash) when the time is right before the market begins to sell their coins in a fearful frenzy. People need to park investments in various places, this ensures that if you put your money in crypto, you'll have other places to look for revenue if Bitcoin decides to tank one day. There are too many analysts who keep saying Bitcoin is in a bubble here in the final months of 2017. They say this each day as the currency climbs, so be careful when it comes to investing in Bitcoin because it is at an all-time high; it is pricier than it has ever been period. This bearish sign doesn't necessarily bring bears into the market unless people start selling their holdings.

Another thing to note, is that Bitcoin may follow historical trends, such as the stock market crash in 2008, but the currency is extremely new to the world and only ten years old. For the bears out there, you might want to watch your words before you wish Bitcoin to crash and burn; you may be out of the play too early due to your pessimism.

When it comes to mood, sometimes it is just better to be an optimist. Like we said, to help you not freak out too much, set a limit as to what percentage you are okay losing.

We also must warn you that *Coindesk* does not offer sell limits, their technology is just not there yet, though they have hired more staff members and engineers for support. So hypothetically, if Bitcoin ends up tanking one day, which falls into the theory; know that everything up must come down and vise-versa. If this is ever the case, you'd better start reaching into the *Coinbase* platform quickly, doing so will minimize your losses; as the stop loss option is not available.

This fact currently causes more fear among investors everywhere.

One more thing, not everything in the world is perfect. *Coindesk* actually has limits on how much you can withdraw and sell at a time, so there are restrictions, which is another limitation. Sure sending and receiving the cryptocurrency transaction is free, but this does not mean that investors are free from being charged for international fees, and exchange fees, being that *Coinbase* runs one of their payment processing offices out of London. There are plenty of pros and cons as you can see, but luckily, you the investor, and you are not limited when it comes to cryptocurrency exchanges. There are other platforms on the market that are competition, (we listed them in the text above). Just think of it this way, all of the profit you make, there will always be fees somewhere, whether it is taxes or an exchange platform charging you for their services; we just can't change this. It is kind of like the old saying, there are two things you cannot change, death and taxes.

Since we all die, who doesn't want to become a millionaire to experience the wealth that you were never able to? With cryptocurrency, you may be that much closer to your goals.

Emerging Markets

It seems that after Bitcoin was able to pass $10K, other markets in the crypto market have also began to take off. As we have mentioned multiple times in this book, don't buy into Bitcoin at such a high price unless you can afford to lose over $20K. If you are looking to become a millionaire off of crypto, then we highly suggest that you start looking into new and emerging cryptocurrencies that also use the blockchain technology, this is what you need to start looking for. Otherwise, you are missing out on the entire concept. Be careful though, as there are many scammers and phishing sites that are ready to prey on vulnerable individuals on the internet as previously discussed. As of December 19, 2017, Forbes online publication mentions that a new cryptocurrency titled Verge

(XVG) has managed to rise to over 800% in a week span [6].

As you can see, when you dip into the arena of cryptocurrency, you will begin to realize that the market moves with incredible turbulence and the market volume causes quick surges that are up and down. This market does not create residual income. Participating in this new market is similar to dating a bi-polar individual.

This new market for digital currency may be a fun ride until the tide has swept you up, and you are experiencing a bearish day. As long as you take the down days with a grain of salt, you will be able to thrive into the future with the cryptocurrency that you are holding.

Remember, if you feel like making a very illogical decision, crack this book open and learn that you

---

[6]

https://www.forbes.com/sites/jessedamiani/2017/12/19/crypto-watch-verge-xvg-price-climbs-800-in-a-week-what-is-xvg-and-why-is-it-growing-so-fast/#18b08ffd444e are really investing in blockchain technology, a type of technology that puts the people in control, rather than the 'big man banks', the currency is also good to transfer currency across borders with very little hassle.

Once you can realize these are the true underlying values that make-up the build of cryptocurrencies than you can start logically seeing the value within. After you do this, you will most likely feel a refrain from clicking on the sell button. We live in a fast and ever-changing world, cryptocurrency is able to keep up with the world that turns 24/7. Just think of it this way, the normal stock market starts at 9 am and ends at 4:30 pm EST, this type of investing is limited. It is obvious that investors like to invest around the clock. Minds tick every second the clock does, making cryptocurrency that much more valuable.

Cryptocurrency Jobs In The Tech Sector

If you love cryptocurrency so much, that you need to work for it, then we highly suggest that you start your career in this type of industry. Think of it this way, the money you earn in the field, you can eventually buy cryptocurrency and perhaps you may have insight on the crypto world because you chose to immerse yourself into this digital asset filled with numbers.

Cryptocurrency assets are very young, and they have yet to show us their full potential. As of now, the digital currency is on the stage and we are the spectators waiting for an ultimate surprise. Technology and finance professionals can now utilize their eagerness to live, breathe, and work with blockchain technology, with startups and companies that are already well-known. This currency has been creating a whole new sector of jobs. You can earn millions by participating in this method and carefully investing your work profit. The jobs that are available, according to a post by Forbes magazine include [7] : Miners, Software Developers, Technical Product Managers, and Consultants. The job descriptions are very technical but have the ability to change as the crypto globe continues to evolve with new modifications and grow from past issues. As we know, upgrading our computers to keep them running at an optimal level is important for security purposes. Technology software is the same way, there always needs to be a better and faster version available in order to succeed. The individuals in these positions will have to evolve with the work duties, as it may have a huge possibility to change along the way, anything is possible with cryptocurrency.

---

[7]

https://www.forbes.com/sites/laurencebradford/201 7/12/18/how-cryptocurrency-has-introduced-new-careers-in-tech/#11e5c94f3e79

Since this is a rather new industry, companies will not expect all new hires to know every single thing about cryptocurrency, it is just not possible yet. If you want to get into this industry, then we highly suggest that you read up all you can on this type of currency—the digital currency which may soon change the way the world exchanges currency. Why not work with something you are entirely passionate about? A good place to start, if you are yearning to work in this newly carved out field, is by taking a class at Princeton University, take the Bitcoin and Cryptocurrency Technologies course.

Who knows, if you get a job in this sector, they may give you some coins, as part of the package.

Digital Coins Advance

Coins change because as we have said, something newer and faster comes out and hits the market with a grand slam. The general population is looking for faster processing and transaction times, Bitcoin remains slow, but is the first well-known cryptocurrency that exists. The fact that Bitcoin is a noteworthy coin, we foresee this coin keeping its value, not only for blockchain purposes, but for reasons that extend to Bitcoin being the 1st digital coin on the market.

Everyday we turn on the news, and a new cryptocurrency is surging. The reasons behind this is because the currency is perceived as being not only fresh but more technologically advanced. As we may have been able to see, cryptocurrency began after the advent of the internet. If there was no internet or online world, then you could kiss this currency goodbye, which is another reason why this currency will never dominate the finance market.

Perhaps it will come close and you can still make millions by learning everything about cryptocurrency that you possibly can, and implementing the logical strategies that we have outlined in this book to carry out your success, but keep in mind, if the internet goes out, you would have zero digital currency to trade.

In order to become a millionaire in cryptocurrency, you have to be smart enough and you have to know when a good time to get out is. Since crypto is only a decade old, it may be wise to tread lightly, as in, invest low in the beginning and minimize your long-term risk. The key here is to research so well that you will have a large inclination and know which alternative cryptocurrency will pop the next day.

Once you move forward with this type of currency, you have to promise yourself that you will not get too caught up and that you will not place all your funds in a cryptocurrency account. We have to say this, as there has been people who invested their entire life savings and ended up homeless because of an all-in type of investment gone wrong.

There Is Always A Dark Side When It The Crypto Craze

When people buy stocks, options, and bonds, they usually choose the company because they believe that the company will grow. For instance, if a person invested in Netflix, they know that Netflix sure does have competitors, but the company has plenty of room to grow, as it is one of a kind. The investors knew what they were signing up for, as they had a good look at the fundamentals and technicals beforehand. The investors were able to see a clear picture for the most part. When it comes to the crypto craze, investors do not have much to work off of, other than speculation. Think about it this way, the industry is new, there are always new alternative digital coins hitting the market, and investors and speculators don't really know if the digital currency is going to stay for the long run.

The plus sides that speculators and investors have, is the blockchain technological software, there are no transaction fees, just exchange fees on platforms like *Coinbase,* the currency is also easy to transfer to different countries, and there is no centralized middle-man intervening like the bank normally does. These are all of the factors that investors see a plus side in.

Of course, if the person's emotions believe in cryptocurrency as a future currency, their emotion is considered not logical, hence giving the investor a sense of 'playing the lottery'. As anyone knows, if you don't play the lottery, how will you ever win? The same question arises with cryptocurrency, if you don't buy Litecoin or Bitcoin, you could possibly miss out on profits and funds.

Fear of loss is always a huge concern for the general population, which is highly understandable and valid. Although, for those investors who do not want to deal with the dark side of investing, then it is smart to avoid cryptocurrency all together. Why avoid it if there is potential to score millions? Because there has been many cases where early investors adopted the digital currency notion and came out very ahead via their bank accounts.

There is a dark side to everything in life, and once you learn all of the aspects that come along with putting your precious hard earned dollars into this new craze, then you can rest at night, knowing it will take time for your money to grow. Learning the downsides and the upsides to your investments can help ease the dark side anxiety that comes with investing in these new digital coins.

More dark sides include hackers, as we keep stressing throughout this book. Hypothetically, what if someone hacked your *Coinbase* account?

Well, if you keep your passwords off of your computer, offline, write it on a piece of paper, store in it a safe, and opt to use *Google Authenticator,* then you should be in better shape. It really is all about securing your assets and your online security. Avoid strange emails and certainly do not click on any strange links, because you may wind up with hacker troubles. A downfall here is that there is no centralized bank to back you up in case if you get hacked. You are on your own in the world of cryptocurrency, which can get lonely.

Check Your Credit Score Often

Not only do we have to be completely cognizant when it comes to our information and all of our assets, but we have to make sure that we check our credit scores often. This way, if there is something that is not correct on our credit reports, then we can report it as soon as we get the real-time notification.

If you want to be a cryptocurrency millionaire, you can't just stop at protecting your coins, you have to make sure to protect every asset that is linked to your name. This is the only way you will get ahead. Sign-up with a reputable company, perhaps Experian instead of Equifax, since Equifax just had a major breach with customers information getting stolen.

Once you are able to see all of the accounts you have open, you may want to print out your report and keep it in a safe place. Make sure to keep your password on these documents as this should also be considered important documents, and saved the same way you treat your cryptocurrency. Upgrade your credit checking abilities and check to see if your information is anywhere on the dark net. Credit checking bureaus finally offer this type of service—dark net. Utilize it, this way you can make sure your coins, your information, and your credit score is correct. If something is not correct, you will need hard evidence to prove that the information is incorrect.

We also highly encourage you to sign-up for the identity theft protection. When you do reach a million dollars after your cryptocurrency grows, you will be thankful you were advised early on.

If something doesn't match up in your credit report, file a dispute, and make a claim. Having daily access to view your credit report costs anywhere between, $9.00-$24.99, depending on the additional services you request. Knowing is always power in your pocket.

North Korea and The Hacking Trend

In the year 2017, America's presidency has changed the stage and appearance of America. Sure the American dollar still goes a long way, but not all tech geniuses, are able to stop North Korea and their ability to hack Bitcoins just yet. North Korea has been threatening the U.S. since the beginning of time. Now that a decentralized market has come to a surface, North Korea is taking cybercrime actions towards various exchanges. They haven't attacked the U.S. as of December 2017, but they have targeted exchanges in South Korea, according to a news article on ABC news[8], posted on December 20, 2017. Apparently, the hackers were able to steal

---

[8] http://www.abc.net.au/news/2017-12-20/north-korean-hackers-raiding-bitcoin-exchanges/9277044

over $5 million dollars in Bitcoin on an exchange in South Korea titled You bit, according to the latest article from ABC news.

North Korea may threaten the U.S. with missiles almost every other week, so cyber attacks aren't uncommon from this country. North Korea, doesn't collaborate with many other countries, hence making it hard to find out who the cybercriminals really are. It is important for cryptocurrency exchanges to recognize that they are a major target, and it is important for these exchanges to keep a tight watch not only on North Korea but all countries.

As long as there is technology, the hacking trend will continue to thrive, as there is a black market for almost everything you can think of. It is a dog eat dog world and criminals in every industry are also looking to make a quick dollar, well in some cases, a quick million.

The internet has been known to be a bit transparent, as people can hide their true identities, this can be argued, but with the evolution of technology and online, newer positions are opening. Individuals who know how to hack for the government, and for purposes of National Security are highly sought after. If you can hack, chances are, *Google* will want to hire you. With this fact alone, it is a given that *Google* works side-by-side with the government. Realize that the government will always monitor what they can, so once cryptocurrency becomes even more mainstream, your coins could become more protected, because if the government can, they too, will make money off of these crimes that cybercriminals are trying to impose on innocent investor victims.

Crypto Criminals

In order for you to be in-the-know with all cryptocurrency news, then you need to be aware, that there are cybercriminals who actually run in gangs 'groups'. For instance, Lazarus is known to be a gang of hackers that have pulled technology heists and bank robberies that go all the way back to 2009. After the U.S., FBI, and NSA conducted deep research, they determined that the hacker group most likely originates out of North Korea, according to ABC news. Sometimes these cybercriminals are so good, they vanish, and leave zero footprints or traces, due to the hackers highly skilled hacking abilities.

Something to be aware of, other countries have the ability to hack exchanges and cryptocurrencies often across a multitude of borders 24/7 as the exchanges never sleep, making this industry global and not national; the key in point is, the more people involved, the more chances a hack can happen. But rest assured, if you have a highly secure exchange and follow the storing methods above than you can rest. Cryptocurrency platforms will try anything and everything from tarnishing their reputation, so chances are they are stopping cyber attacks as you read this book, right this second.

Do Not Forget Your Password

The Washington Post publishes on 12/19/17 [9], that there are plenty of people who are finding their Bitcoins in a type of waiting area as they cannot seem to remember their passwords from long ago. Yes, there are some people who bought Bitcoin a while ago for hundreds or thousands of dollars, who are now millionaires. These people cannot access their Bitcoin's because they have lost their password. As a cryptocurrency holder, it is extremely imperative to know your passwords and security pins that run along with the process of accessing your account.

Of course, trading exchanges have abilities to retrieve lost passwords, but what if the

---

[9] https://www.wsj.com/articles/good-news-you-are-a-bitcoin-millionaire-bad-news-you-forgot-your-password-1513701480

information you entered long ago is no longer saved? Well, then you'll end up unable to retrieve it, as many people are in this current situation. After all, digital currency is decentralized, sure the trading exchanges are beginning to offer more and more services, but at the moment, everything is simply run off the blockchain, which means, you need your own access, because you are the one that started the purchase in the first place; there is no bank to intervene.

The Washington Post also mentions in the same article [10], that Elon Musk apparently reported that he "misplaced part of a bitcoin".

Lately, the price of Bitcoin has constantly been surging to all-time highs as we keep emphasizing; think about how you would feel if you accidentally misplaced your password, and you didn't have a bank to fix your password issue.

---

[10] https://www.wsj.com/articles/good-news-you-are-a-bitcoin-millionaire-bad-news-you-forgot-your-password-1513701480

You'd be missing out on your opportunity to collect your profits if you wanted to sell. You'd better think hard, and you'd better hold on to dear life to your cryptocurrency passwords, or you will be devastated if the price inflates and you become a Bitcoin millionaire, well, sort of. You don't want to be locked out of your chance to be a millionaire if this happens.

If your funds are in some type of waiting room, then you need to think really hard about how you can retrieve your password, otherwise, assets that have been sitting there for a very long time could be vulnerable to a hack.

Some say to store your wallets in a third-party wallet, although this isn't always your best bet. You really need to make sure that the provider you choose to store your digital security on is up-to-date, and has the monetary means to pay for high-end security.

Either way, you need to know you are taking a risk. As we mentioned previously, don't forget to unlink your bank account once you have made a deposit or withdrawal a transaction—this is yet another safety feature you can do for your own peace of mind.

Conclusion

It is always a good idea to look into new markets. In the year 2017, just sign into your everyday stock accounts, sure some of them have grown at a steady pace, this is a given, and a fairly safe method for anyone and everyone who has done their appropriate and due diligent research, but the growth is probably not exponentially.

With new digital assets taking over markets and growing 100% in a matter of hours and 1000% in a matter of months, we should all be able to see which markets and industries are climbing to the top. It is always a disappointment when a person makes an analysis and it turns out to be true, but they don't take the initiative to do something and invest. Don't be the person who said Bitcoin or Litecoin is going to go up if you are not going to get in the game. It is simple, either get in or get out.

Granted, investors who are truly shy, should stay away from cryptocurrency because after all, the market is truly bold and bullish, there is no bank to back you up. So at the end of the day, make sure to properly protect your assets. If you are wondering when the right time to invest in is, the right answer is to look at the technical charts and try to find the currency on a down day. Using this strategy and putting it into play is one of the smartest moves anyone can do.

Of course, people are afraid of the unknown. But, keep in mind it is important that we as humans allow innovation to enter our lives. Making bold choices and taking calculated risks can, in fact, have some long-term glory and wealth. So it is important not to stick to old investing habits, as time changes, and so does the way in which we invest. We need to get out of the mindset that we need to invest slowly and save each paycheck as much as we can, otherwise we are automatically setting ourselves up for low future funds.

It is important to look outside of the box and try new things. Innovation always creates new millionaires. Think about it, old money and new money exist for certain reasons. Take Facebook, for example; there are some people who invested in Facebook when it was on the stock market for less than $30.00 dollars. These tech investors never knew that the Facebook stock would reach $180.00 in December of 2017. If they invested the right amount, then they could now be millionaires too, due to the technology risk they took by investing in a new company—this kind of investor is known to be—a 'new money' investor.

Don't be afraid when you are entering new territory. What investors need to start doing is being bold and certain. The only way investors can start to grip this kind of mental attitude is by learning the in's and out's of whatever it is they are investing in. Sure, cryptocurrency is all over the media as we speak, but let's speculate what we will have once 21 million Bitcoin's have been distributed and there is no more to pass around? What will happen? Of course, the value will go up, and the demand will be higher. So it is highly possible that one day, one Bitcoin will be worth over a million dollars. Once this happens, people will then go to the next currency in line.

The next currency in the line of Bitcoin is Litecoin. Litecoin is practically the brother sibling to Bitcoin, coining itself the silver to Bitcoins gold. It is imperative to study cryptocurrency on a daily basis because there is no telling what will come of the cryptocurrency market. If people buy and use it, the currency will become a hit, if not, the currency will surely take a turn down south. There is a 50/50 percent chance for people all around the world to adopt cryptocurrency. Digital currency is not a fad, it is here to stay, especially in the wake of the advent of the internet.

Technology and solutions improve day by day, the only thing slowing down here is old money. There has never been a better time to invest in new money.

Of course, technology changes every single day, in fact, it changes so fast these days that it is hard to keep up with. Cryptocurrency on the market is extremely volatile. It is so risky to invest at such a high price, so we recommend that if you are looking to invest in coins such as Bitcoin, look to Litecoin, as buying on the low end will always prevail.

Thankfully, some of you out there were able to buy these coins under a thousand dollars or perhaps under five dollars! If you fall into this category than it is positive that you were meant to hit the jackpot when it comes to crypto coins, congratulations. It is not easy to tell whether an investment will go up or down, but it is always more rational to use logic over emotion, as every investor needs to be aware of this major piece of advice when looking to add your hard earned dollars into a growing pot.

Of course, the entire concept that people are fearful to miss out on this grand opportunity still holds its truth. Who wouldn't want to make a million dollars off of Bitcoin or any altcoin? The risk is there, there is the technical analysis that you should carefully watch before your funds go plummeting or before your coins go to the moon and back.

In today's world, 2017, it seems as if traditionalists are 'trying' to stay out of the cryptocurrency picture. Not for long though, as new money arrives and is distributed among thetehcnology driven entrepreneur millennial types of society.

Taking risks has proven to be well for some, while others have managed to lose everything. Don't be that person and always make sure to invest wisely. You need to make sure that you carefully tread as the water and stakes are really high.

If you have the funds, want to take a $18K risk, then, by all means, go for it. With proper calculations, and watchful thinking, you can minimize your risk, but you have to be quick. Bitcoin and all cryptocurrency move quicker than you can say the word quick.

It has been factual that Bitcoin has fallen and risen very abruptly in a matter of minutes or perhaps even seconds. When Bitcoin falls, it can leave you with a $3K loss, just as fast as you can gain $5K in your *Coinbase* account. The world of crypto is very exciting and all of the tech geniuses saw value in the coins early on—a decade ago.

Mainstream has now made alt. coins very unstable here in the last month of December 2017, especially Bitcoin. This is why the market is looking into Bitcoin alternatives. The question is, which alternative digital currency will reign king in the long-term? Bitcoin sure does look like gold right now, considering 21 million total will be in circulation.

The weather is hot and cold when it comes to cryptocurrency. It can be bullish or bearish. At the end of the day, you need to invest in something you believe in. If you believe in this new age type of digital currency like all of the tech nerds did when it first came out, then it is possible that you could be a millionaire by now. Perhaps you already are a millionaire from Bitcoin, the coin keeps going up and up, which makes Bitcoin king when it comes to crypto. Of course with new innovations, there will always be a sense of uncertainty.

Now that the IRS is starting to gain an in into cryptocurrency, this fact gives the digital currency a sense of being more accepted. As mentioned above, the more accepted this type of currency becomes, the more the price will rise in value. Bitcoin is in the news every single day and there is no stopping it. As you read throughout the book, Bitcoin is not the only cryptocurrency around, there are plenty of other currencies that have the opportunity to explode, the same way Bitcoin did.

Fear will continue to surround the crypto world as long as it exists, simply because the currency is still in infant stages. Due to this fact, 50 years from now, Litecoin holders could either be zeroed out or could buy a house with 2 coins, who knows.

Our globe is changing as politics change with new leadership and dictators, this fact leads to a change in the financial world since most of the notable figures and decision makers are paired with banks. Cryptocurrency is taking the dictatorship out of the government and out of banks, and placing finance into the consumer/ investors hands; which is how it should be. There isn't a doubt that digital currency is finance of the future.

The future is full of innovation and advancement, if you take heed of the advice given in this book, you could find yourself a self-made millionaire in 10-20 years from now. Listening is one of the best tools we can be given in the game we call life.

It is up to you, the individual to change the way you live. If you really want to be a cryptocurrency millionaire and think about this everyday, plus you take all of the steps that you need to, you will be on your way to achieving this type of success in no time.

Sooner than later, once you achieve your goal, you can finally look back and say that this book nudged you in the right direction. Feel free to share this book with your friends and family. Why not share knowledgeable wealth? It is one of the best things you can possibly do for a loved one. Remember the saying, teach a man to fish? He'll be able to eat for a lifetime. Now, ask yourself, do you feel more educated in the new realm of cryptocurrency? If so, go out there, read more, acquire more knowledge about crypto-currency coins, and soon you will reach the million dollar mark that you have always dreamed of.

Don't invest out of fear, always invest out of logic, this is the only way you will come out ahead.

Remember, once you reach your monetary goal, you need to be grateful and humble, because remember, when we are no longer on this earth, we cannot take any material possessions with us. So it is best to use your new income wisely. Perhaps spend your profits on new experiences and help out family members if you can. These types of investments are well worth it. Remember when to get out and never get too greedy, otherwise you can lose your funds so quickly, that you don't know what happened.

Happy investing and keep a close eye on new cryptocurrency happenings.